American IN *Paris*

American IN *Paris*

Lessons from the Paris School of Flower Design

MICHAEL GAFFNEY

FLORA PUBLISHING

DESIGN: Rudy Ramos
EDITOR: Kerry Bennett
PRINTED: China

ISBN 978-0-9899258-3-9

PUBLISHED BY
Flora Publishing
PO Box 170004
Whitefish Bay, WI 53217

Table OF Contents

This book is dedicated to all my students who inspire me every day.

Introduction

_H_ello, my name is Michael Gaffney. I'm a designer, educator, writer, and inventor. This book, _American in Paris_, is about my experiences in Paris and how they influenced my work and my career.

My first trip to Paris was several years ago. We all have romantic and visual ideas about what Paris should be, but I had little expectations about seeing Paris other than viewing the Eiffel Tower.

I arrived in Paris and rented an apartment in the Marais section of the city. Every day, I would rent a bicycle outside my apartment building and pick a new direction to cycle in.

What struck me about Paris was the beauty, the beauty everywhere. Every street corner, every railing, every door, every window, every planter box was beautiful in Paris. I spent several days riding in different directions, and I never saw anything that was not beautiful in all of Paris.

That experience inspired me to create more beauty; to realize that the world is filled with people who insist on and create beauty.

I used to joke that they must have put to death anyone in Paris who did not make beautiful things, because everything I saw was so pleasing to the eye. It reminded me of floral design in that everything has to be beautiful and everything has to create emotion when presented to someone-- the best floral designs do, anyway.

So my trip to Paris was more than what I expected. I spent every day on that bicycle, taking in the visual beauty of this great city.

This book is going to talk about the influences, my educating, designing, and all things having to do with the floral experience.

Thank you,
Michael Gaffney

French Lessons

I was so inspired by the beauty of Paris that it almost shifted my viewpoint on floral design. It made me take a more historical, more refined approach to my designing.

Flower designing should be pleasing to the human eye in every way. When someone looks at a flower design arrangement, they don't analyze it and think about it—it's automatically "ooh-la-la, I love that!"

Different designs produce different effects, but all great flower designing should create emotion that makes people heal, love, forget, forgive, remember, honor. The way I see it, flower design is a form of communication. That's why so many people use flowers to communicate their feelings when they can't.

Design principles are important in flower designing—in fact, in every flower design you show me, I will point out the chess moves the designer used to "check mate" to create beautiful designs based on design principles.

The designs you'll see in the following chapter, "French Lessons," are very easy, very do-able designs with great results. The flowers used in the arrangements are available in nearly any market, not just in Paris, and you'll see that much of the importance of the design is in the container.

Enjoy—and keep bloomin'!
Michael Gaffney

This arrangement is a beautiful collection of hydrangeas and roses done in a mass design. I start with the hydrangeas and add our other flowers, angling them almost sideways across the bouquet, which gives it a dome shape. At the end, we add a little bit of ivy for that beautiful cascade and drop it in a very pretty silver urn. This is a quick but lovely design, suitable for any and every occasion.

> *Fashions fade,*
> *style is eternal.*
> — Yves Saint Laurent,
> French fashion designer

Here I have a monochromatic viewpoint, inspired by YSL. Lots of pinks – spray roses and full-size roses, with a little bit of waxflower. By the way, did you know the waxflower is part of the myrtle family? This bouquet is also done in that nice dome shape, with the greenery grevillia added at the end. Greens are a very hot trend, by the way. They easily incorporate a natural, rustic look into your arrangement. This is a fantastically simple design, very fashionable, and suitable for many occasions. We dropped it into a contemporary vase to counterbalance its more traditional style.

Let us be grateful to the people who make us happy; they are the charming gardeners who make our souls blossom.

— MARCEL PROUST, FRENCH NOVELIST

We took this enchanting cobalt blue vase, added hydrangeas and white roses, and found some dark-colored berries to accentuate, or collar, our design—just like a shirt collar. It's like adding a perimeter or outlining your design with another material. Very effective use of a few varieties of flowers, with the berries topping it off. One of the principles of design is unity—bringing the color of your vase up into the arrangement. So here we have a blue vase and some privet berries.

Picasso was born on the border between Spain and France and spent much of his life in France. This arrangement was inspired by him. It's an old-world-looking piece with a lot of drapery and cascading, very dramatic. Here we've used hydrangeas, roses, an olive branch, seeded eucalyptus, and more to create this cascading effect. Then we set it on top of a glass pedestal. Great for an entryway or the middle of a buffet table.

*I want death to find me
planting my cabbages.*

— MICHEL DE MONTAIGNE, FRENCH PHILOSOPHER

The hot new item in the market is kale. For this arrangement, we took kale, collared it with a little waxflower and a little plumosa fern, and dropped it into our concrete urn. As you see, I survived this design! However, it was so easy and very effective; one of my favorite designs in the book.

What a great way to put together calla lilies and dusty miller. Each color of calla lily was bunched together, angled against each other to create the dome, then collared with dusty miller, and dropped into a pretty container. The contrast of the white, pink, and dark purple calla lilies makes an excellent spectrum of color, simple and elegant like Miss Chanel.

Luxury is in each detail.
— HUBERT DE GIVENCHY,
FRENCH DESIGNER

This arrangement is what I call a little bit of everything in my garden, and it's a little bit more difficult. The first thing I do is set the parameters of the size of my design, so I know how wide, how tall, and how round it will be. Then I fill it with all the flowers of my garden. It's wall to wall beauty, with results that are stunning. It reminds me of Givenchy and his fashion collections.

Here I added a cascade effect to a collection of hydrangeas, roses, and berries. This cascading effect is achieved by using anything with a line to it. A cascade is long, instead of round like a mass material. Hydrangeas, roses, and berries go together perfectly in this arrangement. We've added an accent of lily grass to complete the cascade, then set it on top of a beautiful silver vessel.

Here is another lovely garden collection of berries, roses, and fillers all together in a beautiful garden bouquet, representative of a Matisse painting. Simple to do—again, just angle your flowers in a criss-cross fashion from left to right through the center. That's how you create the dome. Hopefully you're seeing that flower design is mostly architecture.

La vie en rose (Life through rose-colored glasses).

— Edith Piaf, French singer, songwriter, and actress

Another beautiful summer garden collection. This season, I've noticed from fashion shows to flower houses that they're adding lots of drama with dark flowers. Here I added dark scabiosa—also known as the pincushion flower—with pink and white roses and peonies to add a very dramatic effect. La vie en rose, la vie en rose, as the song goes.

> *Love is a rose. Every petal an illusion. Every thorn a reality.*
>
> — Charles Baudelaire, French poet and essayist

In this arrangement, again, I have the contrast of light and dark flowers. It's white roses, hydrangeas, and deep purple scabiosa, all dropped into a concrete urn. Concrete is the new material for containers, and I saw a lot of that in Paris. It reminds us of our history, of things old. Concrete is my favorite new material to work with.

A work of art is an idea that someone exaggerates.

— ANDRÉ GIDE, FRENCH AUTHOR

An urn with lots of flowers. What to do? I clustered and zoned my materials in different sections. I started with my hydrangea, and arranged the other items so each one touches up against the hydrangea—a cluster here, a cluster there. It's like a color block sweater—easy to read, and everyone loves cluster and zoning techniques.

55

Creativity takes courage.
— Henri Matisse, French artist

These vases remind me of the glass and metal Louvre Pyramids by the architect I.M. Pei, in the main courtyard of the Louvre Palace in Paris. What courage it must have taken to put up those pyramids—I was fascinated by them, and these containers remind me of that. Sometimes it's as simple as using a different variety of vegetation in each container and a few stems of cymbidium orchids. Here, simplicity is key.

*The work of art must seize upon you,
wrap you up in itself, and carry you away.*

— Pierre-Auguste Renoir, French artist

Here we have more cascading — in this case, it's called *movement*, where
we have flowers moving in a certain direction. In the finished product,
you can see the flowers "moving," as it were, to the right. I used
Casablanca lilies, mini calla lilies, a little dusty
miller, some varieties of seeded eucalyptus,
all together in a nice bouquet dropped
into a pretty silver urn.

> *People discuss my art and pretend to understand it, as if it were necessary to understand, when it's simply necessary to love.*
>
> – PAUL GAUGUIN, FRENCH ARTIST

For this arrangement, we started out with lines of greenery—you start with the greenery first, then build your structure. Here we have a little cascade and a little movement. Then I added a few flowers, white cymbidium orchids and a few hydrangeas, as our main focal point. So easy to do and so pretty—and on trend right now.

Color is all. When color is right, form is right.
— Marc Chagall, French artist

This is a wonderful collection of pink, orange, and green flowers—bright, fun, and exuberant. Cymbidium orchids, gerber daisies (also called gerbera daisies), and carnations, which are very trendy now throughout Paris, and create a vibrant effect. It's a nice, elegant, old-world feel with a pop of modern color that makes this design sizzle.

In our life there is a single color, as on an artist's palette, which provides the meaning of life and art. It is the color of love.

— Marc Chagall, French artist

A pretty statement piece of hydrangeas, eucalyptus, and more, created for this tall contemporary vase. It's basically a handful of hydrangeas and a few other selections cascading down, all tied up and dropped into this clear contemporary vase. Old meets new in this look.

Cascades are everywhere in this arrangement, and the way we like to do them is without using plastic holders or foam on the end of a ball. This is all natural, like 50 reins of a horse running through your hand. You start with the main focal flower, surround each flower with lots of greenery, and add a cascading effect moving downwards. Any hanging material works great for producing a cascade.

In a great mind, everything is great.

— Blaise Pascal, French mathematician

Containers can be everything. In this case, it's a pretty silver knobbed container. I started with a base of mini green hydrangeas, adding other flowers to hold them in place, including ranunculus and a collection of garden flowers.

A contemporary viewpoint of the world—clustered hydrangeas with some line materials in our branches and dendrobium orchids. Great for a mid-century look; a new modern classic.

Falling Down the Rabbit Hole

*H*ow did I become a floral designer? That's an interesting story. Once upon a time, I was working on Wall Street in New York at a commodities brokerage. I was very unhappy and very discouraged. I didn't like the work and I wasn't making a lot of money—not everyone on Wall Street is a "hedge-funder."

I was living in New York, very unhappy, and my mother was worried about me. I decided to go home to Milwaukee for two weeks for a little holiday. One day I wound up at a flower shop in town. I was chatting with the owner, and she asked me if I was available to drive the delivery truck. Since I always needed extra cash, I agreed to drive the truck for the next couple of weeks.

On the last day, when my vacation was nearly over, I told the people in the
flower shop that I had to leave and return to my "real job" on Wall Street. They
were getting ready for a big event that day, so they asked me to stay a little while
and help them finish the flower arrangements.

I told them I didn't know anything about flowers, but they told me all I had to do was stick one red flower into each green setting. I asked them why they needed one red flower in each green setting, and they told me it was called a "focal point."

And I thought to myself, that's interesting. Before that, I was just delivering these gorgeous flower arrangements that I imagined were created by little artist elves—you know, these floral designers who seemed to create the arrangements effortlessly.

I was thinking, I can't do that; I'm a Wall Street guy. But I stayed an extra hour and half to help them out that day, and I came back the next day and the next. And then I stayed years at that flower shop—six years in all— and that was the beginning of my flower arranging career. I learned all about it there—how to do it, how to buy, how to sell, how to design.

I spent the next four years under the tutelage of a great designer. Then I spent five years on my own, and during that time I realized that I had figured out the "Da Vinci Code" of flower design. And here's what I found out: All flower design is based on a small amount of creativity and large amounts of patterns, formulas, science, architecture, and math. I had cracked the code! I learned how to create great floral arrangements quickly and easily, following the design patterns I had invented.

Early on, I discovered the former Wall Street guy could do it! And I've been doing it for 28 years. I know every aspect of the floral business, from buying and selling, to keeping a client, to designing for weddings and other large events. And I know how to make people happy. I always say that great flower arranging makes people forgive, forget, fall in love, remember, and experience a whole range of other emotions.

MICHAEL GAFFNEY
Photography by Everett Engbers

So, I'm very happy I discovered the flower business. I often wonder what I would have done all these years if I hadn't found flower design.

How would I describe my job? I work in an environment that allows me to be creative. It's fun and it's relaxing. It's like being back in high school in that third period art class that you looked forward to because you could spend the whole time just creating, taking a break from the math and science classes you were required to take.

So that's how I wound up in the flower business. Now I'm an author and inventor. I've invented products and sold them on QVC. I have 15 flower design schools all over the country—from Los Angeles to New York and from Chicago to Miami—as well as schools in London, Paris, and Rome. I've been featured on ABC, NBC, and CBS.

I love what I do, and I love my job. I want you to love what you do and love your job.

My students have had amazing results with the work they've done. I can't believe the talent that comes out of them. Many of them start off better than I did. Of course, I didn't have myself as a teacher then, did I? Just kidding... but their work really is amazing.

I'm so happy I fell down this rabbit hole. It was not the career I had expected to do—in fact, I had never even thought about it. It was by happenstance that I wound up in that flower shop, driving that truck.

I had many people along the way who taught me. The best designers are very open about their knowledge, and they'll teach you everything you need to know. So, I'm grateful to them, and grateful for all my experiences.

I have a great career now—and my mother couldn't be happier! I get to make the world a little more beautiful, one stem at a time.

Collections

*O*ne of the reasons you're a great designer is the great flowers you work with. You need the freshest, brightest, most beautiful flowers of the best quality.

Whether it's the markets in Paris, New York, or Chicago, markets certainly do vary wherever you go. I thought the Paris flower market was remarkable both in its variety and its quality. There are three flower markets in Paris, all beautiful. One of the markets, Le Marché aux Fleurs, has been open since 1808. The other flower markets are the Place de la Madeleine and the Place des Ternes. Parisians come here to buy flowers for their balconies and for their homes.

Stateside, I think the greatest flower markets are often found in California because the flowers are grown there. If you have a chance, go to the Carlsbad, Los Angeles, and San Francisco flower markets. I think they're as good as the Parisian markets I went to.

Parisians buy their flowers on a daily basis, I swear. The average European buys flowers much more often than the average American. However, buying more flowers indicates you're enjoying the quality of good flowers. You'll buy them more often and see them as a good purchase, a good value, and a worthwhile stop on your shopping trip.

The flowers that were available in the markets today are many of the same flowers that I've been buying for more than 25 years. New varieties of roses as well as flowers such as anemone and ranunculus have appeared in the markets that weren't there a decade ago—and new colors of roses strike me as the biggest changes in the varieties offered by the markets.

Choosing Flowers for Your Designs

When choosing flowers, I always say, the more classic they feel, the better they are. I'm often in the flower markets, squeezing the flowers like Mr. Whipple. When you feel the flowers, they should be very firm, almost like plastic. That means you're feeling water. Flowers are water with a little color on top, so firmness is the key.

Also, look at the stems. If the greenery is fresh and firm, that means it's a good flower. Roses, of course, should be slightly opening, never tight. The small, tight roses called "bullets" are not grown much anymore—I didn't see any in the Paris markets. Roses should always be slightly unfurled, because they're more mature and they're going to open up and sit on your table for at least a couple of weeks. The best roses are long-lasting.

So, I have my "workhorse" flowers that I work with most often; they're the flowers that hold up the best. You can see many of them throughout this book.

Preserving Your Flowers

There are five steps to preserving your flowers for weeks, instead of days:

1. Choose good flowers.

2. If you want your flowers to last another week, submerge the blossoms under water for 30-45 minutes.

3. Put a couple of drops of bleach in the water, because bacteria forms, shutting down that stem, which serves as the "drinking straw" for the flower to drink up the water.

4. Use "Crowning Glory," a wax sealant that coats flowers in a waxy substance, sealing in the moisture. It's basically a melted candle in a bottle. You can buy it from my website.

5. Cut your stems by two or three inches every few days and refresh the water. Your flowers will last longer than you ever knew they could.

I've had students approach me and tell me how surprised they were that flowers could last two to three weeks. I've often had flowers last up to six weeks in my home.

Flowers can be a long-lasting purchase. I know many people in America, at least, think flowers only last about five days, on average. In Paris, they seem to have a little more faith in their flowers. The average answer I got there was ten days. I'm telling you they should last two to three weeks, minimum, depending on the variety.

Buying Flowers at the Markets

The hardest thing about buying at the flower markets is knowing how much the flowers should cost. The markets in Paris have prices; others are wholesale markets where prices aren't listed.

The only way to get to know the prices of flowers is to visit the markets. When you're new at it, keep a notebook and write down the varieties and what they cost. Flowers are pretty much the same price all year, although they may increase slightly around a holiday.

Paris has a fantastic flower market that offers nearly every flower available commercially from around the world.

It takes experience to choose which flowers work together as well as which colors, but that's the fun of being a flower designer! You're always learning and you're always sharpening your skills. Flower design is about your visual perception of shape and color, so when you see the separate flowers and greenery in the markets, you get better at choosing which ones will complement each other. When in doubt, don't be shy to ask someone at the flower market—they'll give you all the information you need to make great purchases.

Professeur de Fleurs

*O*ften my students jokingly call me "Professeur de Fleurs"—the Professor of Flowers. There I was in Paris, going through the flower markets, feeling like I'd earned the title.

I spent many years learning my craft. A famous actress in my school said to me, "the secret to life is to learn a craft and learn it well—which you have, Michael." Thank you very much!

So, I am a professor of flowers. I teach every angle of the flower business. I often tell my students that flower design is simple. You just need to know a few rules of design, a little math, a little architecture, and throw in a dash of creativity.

My students are my great inspiration. They come to me from all over the country, and most of them know very little about designing when they start class. At the end of the week, after learning 24 styles of design, they can create the most beautiful pieces—some of them are even better than some designers who've been in the business for 10 years.

I don't know how or why it happens—and I don't need to know—but I suspect it's because of their freshness and the fact that they're ingenues in the floral business, that makes their work so spectacular. Every Saturday (the last day of the class), they have this look of shock and amazement on their faces as if they can't believe they've really designed the piece that sits in front of them. It's a very moving experience and a very satisfying one.

I've learned every angle of this business, but I still learn new things all the time Being an expert in floral design allows me to teach floral design around the world. I have many opportunities awaiting me, and I hope to get to all of them one day.

I created my first school in Milwaukee, where I first learned flower design. I now have 15 schools in cities all over the U.S. as well as schools in Paris, London, and Rome. I have truly become the Professor of Flowers!

At my schools, I teach flower design quite differently than it is taught at other schools—or at least I've heard that from my students who have gone to different schools. They tell me that they learned more from me in one day than they learned at another school in two weeks. I'm not bragging; I'm stating the facts. I studied flower design for 15 years before opening my own school. As I used to tell my mother, I could have had two law degrees by now!

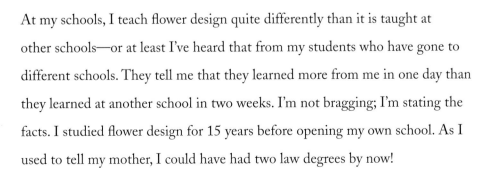

What I came to realize is that flower design is very easy. It's one of the great art forms that nearly anyone can master. I never fail.

Most of my students—and yes, they're mostly women—come to me with the desire to learn a new career, a new trade; to do something they truly love. And I help them get there.

After they graduate they call me, and I help them with placing orders, creating mock-up designs, whatever they need.

My students are my great inspiration. When I'm in class, I feel like I have 10 to 30 mothers sitting there in front of me. The minute I sneeze, they all open their purses and grab cold medicine or a tissue to hand me. It's a really rewarding career. The flower business is lacking great designers, I feel, because everybody went into computers and nursing 10-15 years ago. I get calls every day from companies looking for my students to work for them.

I met so many great designers in Paris and was truly inspired by their work. Many of them have a very solid background in education in design. It was great to see.

My next venture, of course, is my farm-to-table Flower Power. I'm importing flowers from around the world and bringing my classes right into your home. You can now order and watch my classes online for the first time in 14 years.

The flowers will be shipped to you direct—the freshest, brightest, most beautiful flowers! I tell my students that they cannot kill these flowers—they're so fresh, they'll last seemingly forever.

So, there's no excuse not to be a designer; not to walk, talk, and feel like a designer—and create an income by way of flower designing. I've watched many of my students prosper and have strong careers in the floral industry.

I have two other books—*Design Star* and *Flower Power*—which cover many of the design essentials I teach in my classroom.

All those years while I was learning my craft, I thought I ought to be a teacher. My mother, Patricia Gaffney, was a teacher. I remember she used to come home every day when I was a little boy and she had this look of love and satisfaction on her face. As I grew older, I heard other teachers complaining about the teaching industry, but I don't ever remember my mother saying a whole lot. If she ever complained, it was about the parents, not the students.

For me, in the flower industry, I've never had a "bride-zilla." Although I *have* had a "ma-zilla." Typically, brides are in love and they're planning one of the greatest moments of their lives, so they're not difficult and they don't yell at me.

So, I finally got to teach, and I've been doing it now for 15 years. I love my schools, I love my students, and that's why I've dedicated my book to them. Every Saturday on the last day of class, it's the gift they give back to me—their spectacular designs. It takes me back to Paris, where everything was so beautiful, everything was done right, and everything has its place.

Thank you for reading my book. If you haven't gone to Paris, please get there. If you're ever near one of my schools, stop in and say hello.

Au revoir... for now.

Epilogue:
Flower Power

ever forget the power of flowers. They can make people forget, forgive, remember, honor, fall in love, and they can evoke many other emotions. People buy flowers to say what they don't know how to say.

Great design emotes more than just ordinary flower design, so become a great designer—get your flowers to speak, and whisper, for you.

For further information, go to www.buyflowerpower.com or www.flowerschool101.com.

Feel free to go to YouTube and watch the videos from my classes, which show my fantastic students and their creations after they've studied with me. Google "Michael Gaffney" or "American School of Flower Design." I never say goodbye—instead I say see you later and keep bloomin'!

—MICHAEL GAFFNEY

Postcards from Paris

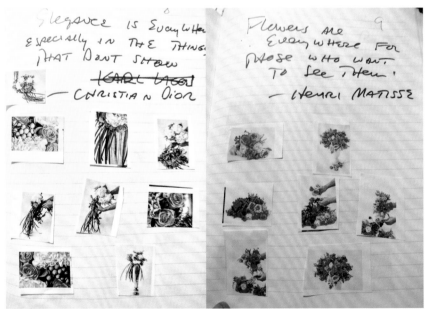

Elegance is Everywhere especially in the things that don't show

— CHRISTIAN DIOR

Flowers are everywhere for those who want to see them.

— HENRI MATISSE

150

MICHAEL GAFFNEY is an author, inventor, entrepreneur, teacher, and designer. He's been studying flower design for more than 25 years. *American in Paris* is his third book. He's also the author of *Design Star* and *Flower Power*.

Mr. Gaffney lectures and demonstrates floral design at museums worldwide and on television programs such as the Hallmark Channel, the Today Show, and QVC. His "Da Vinci code" method of flower design has taught students in 15 American locations the art of design. His most recent business venture is **www.buyflowerpower.com**, where students can order farm-to-table flowers and learn at home. His class and appearance schedule can be found at **www.flowerschool101.com**.